ELEPHANT JOURNEY

The True Story of Three Zoo Elephants
and their Rescue from Captivity

ROB LAIDLAW   art by BRIAN DEINES

pajamapress

An ANN
FEATHERSTONE Book

First published in the United States in 2016

First published in Canada in 2015

Text copyright © 2015 Rob Laidlaw

Illustration copyright © 2015 Brian Deines

This edition copyright © 2015 Pajama Press Inc.

This is a first edition.

10 9 8 7 6 5 4 3 2 1

www.pajamapress.ca   info@pajamapress.ca

The publisher gratefully acknowledges the support of the Canada Council for the Arts and the Ontario Arts Council for its publishing program. We acknowledge the financial support of the Government of Canada through the Canada Book Fund (CBF) for our publishing activities.

Cover and book design—Martin Gould and Rebecca Bender

Original art created with oil paints on canvas

Manufactured by QuaLibre Inc./Print Plus
Printed in China

Pajama Press Inc.

181 Carlaw Ave., Suite 207, Toronto, Ontario Canada, M4M 2S1

Distributed in Canada by UTP Distribution
5201 Dufferin Street, Toronto, Ontario Canada, M3H 5T8

Distributed in the U.S. by Ingram Publisher Services
1 Ingram Blvd., La Vergne, TN 37086, USA

An Ann Featherstone Book

Library and Archives Canada Cataloguing in Publication

Laidlaw, Rob, author
    Elephant journey / Rob Laidlaw ; art by Brian Deines.
Includes index.
ISBN 978-1-927485-77-4 (bound)

    1. Captive elephants--Canada--Juvenile literature.
2. Wildlife rescue--Canada--Juvenile literature. 3. Animal sanctuaries--California--Juvenile literature. I. Deines, Brian, artist II. Title.

SF408.6.E44L33 2015   j599.670971   C2015-902382-3

Publisher Cataloging-in-Publication Data (U.S.)

Laidlaw, Rob, 1954-
    Elephant journey : the true story of three zoo elephants and their rescue from captivity / Rob Laidlaw ; art by Brian Deines.

[40] pages : color illustrations, color photographs ; cm.

Includes index.

Summary: "An illustrated true account of three ailing elephants' journey from a cold Canadian zoo to a sanctuary in California, where they were healed by the warmer climate and more suitable terrain" - Provided by publisher.

ISBN-13: 978-1-92748-577-4

1. Captive elephants - Canada - Juvenile literature. 2. Wildlife rescue - Canada - Juvenile literature. 3. Animal sanctuaries - California - Juvenile literature. I. Deines, Brian. II. Title.

599.67091 dc23   SF408.6E44L343 2015

Photo Credits

Page 3: Iringa enjoying life at PAWS—photograph courtesy of Lisa Worgan/Performing Animal Welfare Society | Page 36: Elephant in Profile-photograph courtesy of Jo-Anne McArthur | Page 36: close-up of legs, feet, toes, and trunk-Shutterstock ©Villiers Steyn | Page 36: Elephant eating a thorn bush-Shutterstock ©Marie-Anne Aberson | Page 36: African Elephant Eating-Shutterstock ©Tim Ridgers | Page 37: Toka at the Toronto Zoo-photograph courtesy of Jo-Anne McArthur | Page 37: Iringa and Toka at the Toronto Zoo-photograph courtesy of Jo-Anne McArthur | Page 37: A herd of elephants in Tanzania-Shutterstock ©GTS Productions | Page 38: Elephant investigates a crate-photograph courtesy of Zoocheck | Page 38: Loaded flatbed truck-photograph courtesy of Zoocheck | Page 38: Crate being lifted off truck-photograph courtesy of Zoocheck | Page 38: Elephant rear end in crate-photograph courtesy of Zoocheck | Page 38: Trunk reaching out of crate-photograph courtesy of Zoocheck | Page 38: Trunk resting on crate window-photograph courtesy of Zoocheck | Page 39: Iringa at the Toronto Zoo-photograph courtesy of Zoocheck | Page 39: Toka and Iringa at PAWS-photograph courtesy of Lisa Worgan/Performing Animal Welfare Society | Page 40: Thika at PAWS-photograph courtesy of Lisa Worgan/Performing Animal Welfare Society

Dedicated to the memory of Pat Derby,
a tireless advocate for elephants and other animals.

    — R.L.

To Iringa.

    — B.D.

Iringa enjoying life at PAWS

Toka, Thika, and Iringa stood together on a small, barren hill. The three friends had no place to roam about, no trees to explore, and no pasture to graze. Every day was the same as the day before. Only the weather changed. Sometimes it was hot; other times it was icy and cold.

When they were babies, Toka and Iringa roamed with their families in the warm, dry climate of southern Africa. They explored a vast territory, with hills to climb and streams to cross. They foraged for grasses, fruit, branches, and bark.

Like all wild elephant females, Toka and Iringa would have stayed with their mother and family group their whole life. Their male brothers would eventually leave to create their own groups and find other females. But Toka and Iringa were captured and brought to a zoo in Toronto, Ontario, Canada. Thika was born at the zoo nearly ten years after they arrived. She never lived in the wild.

The zoo in Toronto was nothing like southern Africa. The ground was hard and dry, and uncomfortable on their feet. The enclosure was too small to roam about, so without enough exercise, the elephants gradually became weaker and out of shape. And it was cold in the winter, too frigid for elephants used to the warm sun of southern Africa.

Like other zoo elephants before them, the three friends were showing signs of ill health. When she got older, Iringa even had trouble lying down and standing up on her own. People began to worry that Toka, Iringa, and Thika might not live past their early forties, which is just past middle age for a wild African elephant.

The Toronto Zoo decided to send the three elephants away to another zoo. But animal protection groups appealed to the city to choose an animal sanctuary in California called PAWS (Performing Animal Welfare Society), where many animals are protected after living in zoos and circuses.

The trip to California could be risky for the elephants, so the plan was to move them as quickly as possible. But they had to drive three crates on two flatbed trailers more than 2,500 miles (4,100 kilometers). Animal welfare groups had crates constructed for Toka, Iringa, and Thika. While the three elephants became accustomed to spending time in their new crates, the final arrangements were made for their trip.

On October 18, 2013, the rain poured down while a giant-sized crane lifted the three crates onto the flatbed trailers. Loading three 4-ton elephants was slow work, and it wasn't until that night that the trucks inched out of the zoo grounds and onto the highway. The trucks were followed by a camper van, where elephant welfare experts monitored the elephants' condition with special cameras.

After a few hours, the trucks arrived at the border crossing between Canada and the United States. The officials couldn't believe what they saw, but as soon as they understood the situation, they wished the group well and passed the trucks through the border.

The trucks continued on all through the night and the next day, stopping only to refuel, check, feed, and water the elephants and clean out their waste. Toka, Iringa, and Thika never left the safety of their crates.

Stopping in Illinois and Iowa, they crossed Nebraska and moved up the high plateau of Wyoming, where the temperature quickly dropped. The roads were clear, but an unexpected snowstorm had moved through the area ahead of them and the winds were still fierce. The trucks swayed back and forth on the highway.

Across Wyoming and down into Utah and Nevada they continued. As they approached California, moving up one mountain and down another, the brakes on one truck overheated and smoke began to billow from the wheels. But the driver doused the wheels with water, and after twenty minutes they were ready to continue.

Finally, after the long journey, a small crowd of people greeted the trucks at the PAWS sanctuary. Toka's crate was the first to be unloaded next to the elephant barn entrance, followed by Iringa and Thika's crates. Toka slowly backed out, turned around, and took her first steps into the small outside holding pen and a new life. Iringa followed. Thika, the youngest, was anxious about leaving the crate, but after nearly an hour, she too came out.

Toka soon entered the massive elephant barn. Beyond two large barriers, the three resident elephants, Mara, Lulu, and Maggie, were waiting, trembling with excitement. Soon the barn was full of the sound of roaring, trumpeting, and rumbling as the newcomers were greeted. The elephants stretched their trunks through the barriers and tried to touch each other as they continued to call out. It was as if the elephants were old friends who had been reunited at last.

In the days that followed, the three newcomers got to know their new home. At the zoo in Toronto, their enclosure had been barely one acre of mostly barren ground. Here, eighty acres of natural land was fenced in and ready for them to explore: hills, trees, streams, and grasslands. It was as warm as an African spring. Soon, even Iringa, who was being treated for arthritis, was able to climb some of the hills using muscles she hadn't exercised very much since she was a baby.

A year later, all three elephants are much stronger and healthier. They can climb the steepest hills. They graze in the long grass, browse in the trees, submerge themselves in a swimming hole, take a mud bath, or just go off to be alone. And Iringa can lie down in the warmth of the sun and then get up again, all on her own.

It has taken a lifetime, but at last Toka, Iringa, and Thika have a safe home and the care of people dedicated to their welfare. One day, the gate separating the newcomers from Mara, Lulu, and Maggie will be opened, and all six elephants will roam the habitat as a new family group.

But for now the three friends are content to trumpet a greeting to their neighbors as they bask in the California sun and feel the luxury of soft grass under their feet.

Elephants have evolved to live in the warm climates of Africa and Asia. They can tolerate cool temperatures for short periods, but there is a limit to what they can take. Modern elephants don't have the adaptations for living in the cold that the mammoths and mastodons had before they became extinct.

People who have only seen elephants in a zoo may be surprised to learn that they are one of the most active of all mammals. They are made for movement. In the wild, elephants explore, forage, bathe, socialize, and engage in a broad range of other behaviors and activities for up to twenty hours a day. During times when food is plentiful, they may only travel a few miles each day. But they can inhabit home ranges measuring from tens to many thousands of square miles in size, following long-established travel routes. Elephants can roam through tropical forests, open savannah, mountainsides, river valleys, deserts, or other kinds of complex terrain.

Walking is good for **elephants**. It keeps them mentally stimulated and helps them stay physically fit and healthy, including keeping their feet moist, lubricated, and in good shape, which is critical for elephant health. In addition to walking, elephants also use their feet to push, pull, stomp, and dig as they go about their daily business. But elephants do other things as well, such as grazing in pastures, foraging in bushes and trees—and even using their tusks to scrape the walls of caves to obtain salt, which they need in their diet.

Elephants can eat from 300 to 600 pounds (135 to 300 kilograms) of vegetation every day

Zoos cannot provide elephants with the conditions they were made for. At the Toronto Zoo, for instance, Toka, Thika, and Iringa shared a tiny outdoor space of less than an acre (just 3,356 square meters). It was mostly barren earth with no pasture to graze or trees to pull down. They couldn't walk very far and didn't have a lot to do. Most nights during the colder days of winter, they were confined in a small barn less than 10,000 square feet (920 square meters) in size.

Throughout their years at the zoo, Toka, Thika, and Iringa saw seven **elephants** pass away. The oldest to go was forty-year-old Tarra, who suffered from severe arthritis. She was found dead in November 2009, when her keepers arrived for their morning shift. TW was the youngest. In 1984, at just two months of age, she died, apparently from a heart condition.

Elephants are among the most social of all animals, and females live in the same family group their entire lives. Families may consist of babies, teenagers, adults, and seniors. The oldest, wisest female is usually the leader of the family, and she is called the matriarch. The males go off and live in bachelor groups when they reach their teenage years and then later live on their own.

Female elephants often help new mothers look after their babies. They are called allomothers.

Over time, people became concerned about the **elephants**. They wrote letters to the local newspaper and circulated petitions. The Toronto Zoo conducted a study, and in May 2011, they made a decision to send the elephants to another zoo. Zoocheck, an animal protection charity, and other elephant advocates pushed to send Toka, Thika, and Iringa to the PAWS sanctuary in California instead, a facility with more space and natural terrain than any zoo, and with an elephant-friendly climate.

African elephants can weigh 8,800 to 15,400 pounds (4,000 to 7,000 kilograms), so moving them in crates is a delicate operation

On October 25, 2011, the Toronto City Council voted 31–4 to send the elephants to the PAWS sanctuary, something they were able to do because the elephants were owned by the city. Zoo staff and others fought the decision and caused numerous delays. Just over a year later, they forced the issue back to Toronto City Council. On November 27, 2012, the council again voted overwhelmingly in favor of sending the elephants to the PAWS sanctuary. Opponents to the move kept fighting and caused more delays, but finally, on October 17, 2013, Toka, Thika, and Iringa were loaded onto the trucks, and their journey to California began.

An elephant's trunk has no bones and can bend, curl, and move in any direction. It contains more than 60,000 muscles.

At the sanctuary, Toka, Thika, and Iringa would enjoy eighty acres of grassy fields, hills, gullies, woodlots, and water holes for submerging. No longer would they have to stand around in a barren exhibit or endure the cold Toronto winters. Instead, almost every day they would be outside enjoying the natural terrain and open spaces.

As this book was about to go to press almost two years after the move, Toka, Thika, and Iringa had enjoyed life at PAWS, climbing the the steepest hills, grazing in open pastures, foraging in the trees, rolling in the earth, and basking in the sunshine. For the first time in many years, they were able to live like elephants should.

Sadly, Iringa's long history of degenerative joint and foot disease—the leading cause of death for elephants in zoos—caught up with her and she was humanely euthanized on July 21, 2015. She was 46 years old. Iringa was born in the wild but spent most of her life in zoo captivity. I'm so glad she had a chance at the end of her life to roam the hills, eat natural vegetation, and enjoy a peaceful life in the company of other elephants. Iringa will be greatly missed.

Iringa

ACKNOWLEDGMENTS: The campaign to have Toka, Thika, and Iringa moved to the PAWS sanctuary was long and difficult, and involved a lot of people. Leading the effort was Zoocheck's Julie Woodyer, assisted by the author. Council members Michelle Berardinetti, Glenn De Baeremaeker, Raymond Cho, and Shelley Carroll were passionate elephant advocates at the City of Toronto. Lawyers Doug Christie, Richard Bickelman, and Clayton Ruby dealt with the legal issues, and local activists Linda Bronfman & Everybody Loves Elephants, Steve Gordon, and Gert Zagler helped push the issue forward.

The actual transport of three elephants across the continent was a major task. W.S. Bell Cartage, Infogate Computers Inc., Howard Smith, JSW Manufacturing Inc., W.D. Boat Tops & Interiors, and Superior Crane provided the services and equipment that made it possible. Margaret Whittaker, Scott Blais, Patrick Lampi, Joel Parrott, Jeff Kinzley, Andrea Goodnight, Lisa Worgan, and the author made up the team that traveled with the elephants on their journey.

Special thanks go to animal advocate/television celebrity Bob Barker for his invaluable campaign assistance and for providing funding to move Toka, Thika, and Iringa to California, and to esteemed animal activist Nancy Burnet for her unwavering support for the campaign.

And last, but not least, are Pat Derby and Ed Stewart, the co-founders of PAWS. If it were not for their passion and vision throughout the years, there would be no PAWS sanctuary for the elephants to call home.

Lots of open space at the PAWS sanctuary gives the elephants room to roam

Index

Thika at PAWS